MW01005792

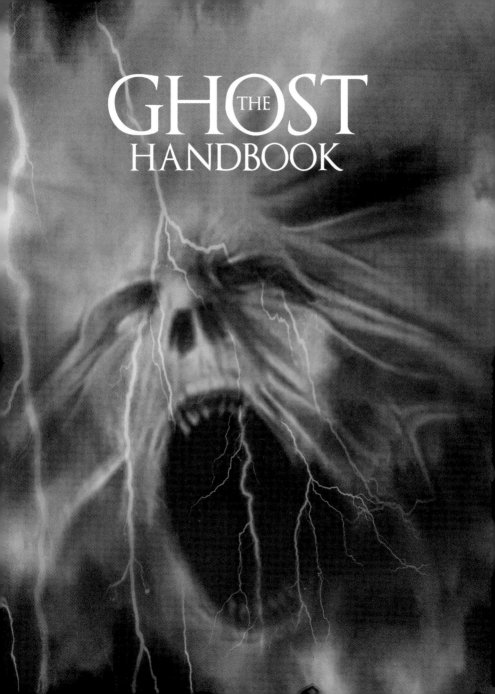

GHOST
THE
HANDBOOK

First edition for North America published in 2011 by
Barron's Educational Series, Inc.

All inquiries should be addressed to:
Barron's Educational Series, Inc.
250 Wireless Boulevard
Hauppauge, NY 11788
www.barronseduc.com

ISBN: 978-0-7641-6456-9
Library of Congress Control Number:
2010942737

M GHHB

Conceived, designed, and produced by:
Marshall Editions
The Old Brewery
6 Blundell Street
London N7 9BH
www.marshalleditions.com

Publisher: James Ashton-Tyler
Creative Director: Linda Cole
Commissioning Editor: Miranda Smith
Editor: Elise See Tai
Design: Tim Scrivens – TJ Graphics
Production: Nikki Ingram

Date of manufacture: July 2011
Manufactured by: 1010 Printing International Ltd.
Color separation by: Modern Age Repro House Ltd.,
   Hong Kong

Printed in China

10 9 8 7 6 5 4 3 2 1

GHOST
THE
HANDBOOK

Dr. Robert Curran

BARRON'S

What Is a Ghost?

The living have always been frightened of the dead. As primitive peoples huddled by their fires, they must have wondered what lay out there in the darkness beyond the comforting glow. Were they haunted by the spirits of dead ancestors?

For many ancient cultures, death was not the end of involvement in the world of the living. The dead were believed by many to remain close by, keeping a watchful eye on those they had left behind – sometimes even intervening in things when they saw fit. Such interventions could be benign – to protect, to warn, to advise – but sometimes it was very different. It was generally thought that the dead envied the living for their earthly pleasures, and that in some cases the dead actually hated the living and sought only to terrify them and do them harm.

The idea that dead ancestors were somehow lurking in the shadows, watching and waiting, often filled the living with a sense of dread. This was made even worse when unexplained events occurred, or strange sounds and sensations were experienced. These events, it was argued, signified that the dead were trying to make themselves known or were trying to influence the living world in some way.

Ghosts are often associated with dark and lonely places. Many reported encounters with them occurred when people were alone and perhaps very vulnerable. Ghosts are also associated with ancient buildings or particular areas – old houses, gloomy castles, remote areas. And it is not hard to understand why. These may be associated with former times or they may have a slightly sinister aspect to them, so they create a feeling of unease. By their natures, they may also be more susceptible to tricks of light and strange noises.

During the medieval period, in the Christian West, the Church often actively encouraged a belief in ghosts. Ghosts, it said, were indisputable proof that there was an afterlife, and that if people did not follow Church teachings they might be denied entry to Heaven, or Hell, and might be forced to wander the world as spirits forever. The idea of the wandering spirits of evil people only added to the terror that was built up around the very idea of a ghost. If it was evil in life, it might be all the more evil in death.

It was during the 19th century, however, that ghosts really came into their own. As new and exciting inventions ushered in a mechanical age, there was still a look back toward the past. Many people

LEFT *Cold, misty woodland areas are perfect places for ghostly encounters.*

More recently, there have been a number of scientific attempts to explain what ghosts might be exactly. Some investigators have suggested that ghosts are "psychic residue" left behind by people, or events in the past that have somehow left an imprint on the fabric of time. Others have suggested that ghosts might be "recordings" that have been absorbed into the surrounding environment and can somehow be "replayed" by those who have the essential psychic ability. This would explain why, they say, some people see ghosts and others do not.

Whatever the true nature of ghosts may be – whether they are spirits of the dead or if there is some scientific reason for them – they have never lost their power to terrify people.

ABOVE *Who knows what ghosts are exactly, but for those that come across them, it is most often a terrifying encounter!*

believed that the past was not really over and still lurked in ancient houses and in eerie valleys. They also believed that the past might take the form of ghosts, and the books and stories of the time reflected this. The idea that spirits were everywhere continued into the early 20th century with the rise of the Spiritualism religion and the continued growth and popularity of ghostly literature.

RIGHT *Some people believe that they are haunted by their dead relatives. What are their ghostly intentions – do they stick around on Earth for good or evil?*

Types of Ghost

For many people, a ghost is a wispy spirit wandering through an ancient house. Or it may be a transparent monk drifting through the ruins of an ancient abbey.

These romantic 19th century notions have been passed down to us through literature and art. The idea of the ghost has changed over the years, and earlier phantoms were thought to be very different. In the medieval period, there seemed only marginal differences between the living and the dead. The dead had bodies and were as solid as the living. They could eat, drink, and engage in activities just like a living person. Indeed, it was believed that the dead rose from the grave at certain times, both day and night, and carried on much as they had done when alive. However, these spirits could be very short-tempered and were not thought to be very well-disposed toward the living, so it was best to avoid them. Ever since these early, bad-tempered specters, people have tended to give ghosts a wide berth.

There are also stories of disembodied spirits among the ranks of the dead who could make their presence known in the living world. These were known as *poltergeists*, a word that comes from two German words – *poltern* meaning to rumble or make noise, and *geist* meaning a spirit. These "noisy spirits" usually attached themselves to either a place or a person and created mayhem. They threw stones, broke crockery, moved furniture, or simply nipped or punched those unfortunate enough to attract them. Many poltergeists might still exist.

There is also another and more dangerous type of spirit – although perhaps the word "ghost" may not strictly apply since they have never actually been born. These are *elementals*, spirits that are made up of raw natural energy or have been born out of an evil deed. They

are thought to be very vicious and can bring physical harm to those unfortunate enough to come into contact with them.

The ghost world, therefore, is not solely made up of drifting, gentle spirits – there are other more vicious powers and forces, too. It is perhaps a good idea to avoid anything to do with ghosts! You have been warned!

RIGHT *We all have a picture of what a ghost looks like in our minds, but what do the real things resemble? Would you like to find out?*

FIRST HAUNTINGS

*There were many ghosts in the ancient world.
The Greeks and the Romans referred to them as
umbrae, which simply means "shade" or "specter."*

Different civilizations divided the ghosts into different categories. The Romans described them as *lares*, good ghosts who were willing to help the living; *lemures*, truly evil ghosts who actually physically hurt the living; and *manes*, who were largely indifferent but were generally good ghosts.

References to ghosts also appear in the works of some ancient writers, such as the *Apocolocyntosis* of Seneca and Pliny's *Natural History*. According to Pliny, ghosts were only the spirits of those who had died prematurely or violently, or both. While these spirits were not necessarily violent in themselves, they were still things that should be avoided.

Ghosts could make their presence known by moaning and wailing, or even reciting long passages of poetry or prose. More often, they might throw stones or bits of earth to create damage and to hurt the living. They were more of a nuisance than anything else. When they were seen, they usually looked like they had when they were alive. They tended to haunt the places that they knew and did not travel very far.

In ancient Egypt, ghosts often appeared as glowing figures that were the spirits of the dead. It was also thought that these spirits, known as *khu* or *ka*, might also live independently of the body. In the later Greco-Roman Egyptian period, the *khu* were considered to be evil.

The entity that corresponded most closely to our idea of a ghost, however, was the *akh*, which often took the form of a bird. The *akh* could reach out far beyond the grave in order to influence events and do good.

The ghosts of the ancient world were a mixture of different spirits. It was only later that they became really threatening and terrifying, striking fear into the hardiest of souls.

ABOVE *In ancient Egypt, some ghosts took the form of birds.*

BELOW *The ghosts of ancient Egypt could have different intentions – good or evil.*

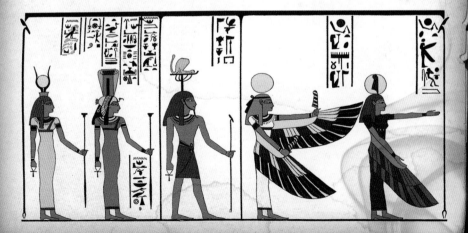

THE DARKENED ROOM

From the middle of the 19th century until the early 20th century, much of western Europe and North America seemed to be gripped by an interest in ghosts.

People believed that there were certain people who could see and talk to spirits. These were the spirit-seers or "mediums." Such people conveyed messages from the spirits in the afterlife to their loved ones in the living world, usually for a fee. The contact was often carried out in questionable conditions, especially in darkened rooms. There is little doubt that some of these mediums were frauds, and that their contact sessions, known as "séances," were bogus.

As time went on, séances became more and more elaborate. Ghosts

spoke, created spiritual "substances" called ectoplasm, sang songs, blew trumpets and whistles, and made objects rise and fall. Some of these mediums – mostly women – made a good living out of their work, and performed in the theaters and music halls. The performances rivaled those of the stage magicians of the time, with the mediums contacting the dead while being bound.

There was a Scottish medium, Daniel Douglas Home, who was said to have been held aloft by ghosts in front of witnesses. Londoner, Agnes Guppy made inert objects move by commanding invisible phantoms to lift them, and Londoner, Florence Cook was supposed to have created a "full-body manifestation" of a ghost known as Katie King, the daughter of pirate John King.

Three of the most influential mediums were the Fox Sisters: Leah, Margaret, and Kate – from Hydesville, New York. They are generally credited with founding the Spiritualist religious movement. As an old woman, Margaret confessed that they were frauds, although she

ABOVE *Medium Helen Duncan conjures up the spirit of a young girl called Peggy during one of her séances.*

later tried to retract the confession. But this did not impact on the movement, which still flourishes.

The last medium of any note was Helen Duncan from Scotland, who was tried and imprisoned under the Witchcraft Act of England in 1944. Her "crime" concerned a séance in 1942 – she had summoned the ghost of a sailor who revealed what was then a wartime state secret – the sinking of *HMS Barham.* But if this was a fraud, as some claimed, how did she come to know a state secret?

LEFT *Séances were carried out to contact spirits in the afterlife and they often took place in darkened rooms.*

GHOST HUNTERS

During the mid to late 19th century, some people claimed that they could contact the dead. There were also people who investigated such claims — these were ghost hunters.

One of the most famous and controversial of these 19th-century investigators was Harry Price, who was born in London in 1881. When he was as young as 15 years old, he claimed to have spent the night in a "haunted house" in order to take a picture of a ghost, but mysteriously, the picture did not come out. As he grew older, he became fascinated by magicians and magic tricks and became a member of the Magic Circle and the Society of American Magicians.

ABOVE *Harry Houdini was a magnificent performer. He used his knowledge to uncover some so-called mediums as frauds.*

LEFT *Ghost investigator Harry Price seated with what looks like a ghostly figure by his side.*

He was then able to use the magic skills and knowledge he acquired to uncover how some so-called "mediums" could play tricks on their unknowing clients.

In 1920, Harry Price joined the Society of Psychical Research. In 1922, he exposed the famous "spirit photographer" William Hope as a fraud. But his main claim to fame is his investigations in Borley Rectory (see pages 54–57). Toward the end of his life, Price worked with a medium named Stella Cranshaw and was himself accused of being a fraud. He died in 1948, still considered a controversial figure.

Another ghost hunter was the Hungarian-born American Erik Weisz, better known as Harry Houdini. A famous illusionist and escapologist, Houdini believed that he had been cheated by mediums following the death of his mother, Cecilia, and set out to expose them as frauds. Like Price, he used his knowledge of how to create illusions in his quest to carry this out. His most famous exposure was that of the celebrated medium Mina Crandon, and this event earned him great fame.

However, Houdini never stopped believing that he might come back from the dead himself. When he died in 1926, he had arranged a secret code with his wife, Bess, that would help her prove that an apparition (ghostly figure) was his ghost. An Official Houdini Séance is arranged every year, but so far he does not seem to have returned to the living world.

GHOST STORIES

There have always been stories of ghosts and the returning dead. These tales inspired awe and terror, and were often used to explain strange shapes glimpsed in the twilight. Such stories were usually connected with the dead, and while they terrified those who heard them, they often fascinated them as well. So it has continued. Everyone, it seems, loves to be frightened by a good ghost story. Now you must turn the pages and prepare to shiver over some of the most frightening stories from the beyond.

BISHOP GERMANUS
AND THE GHOST

One of the oldest medieval ghost stories is thought to have come from France and is to be found in extremely ancient Church records. Although it may be little more than a legend, it was still believed throughout the Christian world right up until modern times.

The frightful tale concerns St. Germanus, Bishop of Auxerre. In 500 A.D., he was traveling across the French countryside with some companions on Church business. Darkness and a windstorm stopped their journey, and so they had to look for shelter close by. There was only one place that they could stay for the night – a dirty and disreputable hovel on the edge of a deep and impenetrable forest. The place had an extremely sinister reputation. It was said to be haunted by a frightening and evil ghost that, according to some local traditions, had driven many brave men screaming from its doors. No one knew any details about the ghost or what the ghost was because nobody had stayed long enough near the place to find out.

Germanus was, of course, a holy man and an important bishop, so neither he nor his companions had any great fear of the ghost. Therefore, they decided to camp in the dreadful place. As they settled down, there was a sudden disturbance. A terrible apparition, a cloud of white mist in the shape of a tall man, rose from the floor and began to pelt them with stones, making horrible groaning and shrieking noises as it did so.

RIGHT *When Bishop Germanus and his companions came across the creepy hovel, they had no choice but to stay.*

The companions were terrified, but Bishop Germanus stepped forward and asked the ghost to stop. It replied by hurling abuse and throwing clods of earth at him. The Bishop then called on the name of the Lord. For a few moments, the ghost only replied with blasphemies, obscenities, and further insults. Then Germanus sank to his knees and began to pray, calling directly on God for His help. At this, the ghost suddenly calmed itself, ceased its foul language, and stopped throwing stones and earth.

Sensing that he now had the upper hand, Germanus demanded to know who it actually was and why it had behaved in such a fashion to those who entered the house. The cloudy figure replied that it was indeed the spirit of an evil man

Right *Bishop Germanus seemed to have no fear when confronted by the physical and verbal abuse of the evil spirit. He used his experience to preach to his fellow Christians about the correct way to be buried.*

who had once lived in the hovel. He had died there, but had not been buried with the proper rites of the Church, so his spirit was trapped in the area and could never achieve the afterlife. As a result, the spirit took out its anger and frustration on all those who visited the place.

The Bishop asked the phantom to show him where its bones had been buried, and the spirit took him to a secluded place a little way into the forest. As soon as the Bishop's companions began to dig in the area, they found human bones, which they carried to a nearby sacred ground. Germanus himself said prayers over the tomb, therefore allowing the spirit to pass to its eternal reward. The Bishop then returned and blessed the hovel at the edge of the forest in order to drive out all unclean and disturbed spirits and the place became quiet once more.

Later, Germanus would preach a great sermon based on the incident, reminding Christian people of the need to be buried according to the rites of the Church, or they, too, would lie unquiet in the grave.

Left *The ghost's human remains were uncovered and were buried properly in order to enable the spirit to reach the afterlife.*

THOROLF HALT-FOOT

In ghostlore, Viking specters are often the most dangerous. They are the ghosts of dead warriors and are very much as they had been in life, although with increased nastiness. They are almost indistinguishable from the living and are only known by their pale white or blue-black faces.

Viking ghosts might appear at any time of the day or night. When they do, they simply take up their old ways: drinking, eating, roistering (making lots of noise), or more than likely, fighting with the living. Many will pick arguments with some innocent person. In some cases in the past, bands of the dead even traveled around the countryside together, terrorizing the living. Gangs of dead warriors would sometimes turn up at the doors of houses demanding to be fed or given strong drink, and the people within would very often be too scared to refuse them.

Scandinavian tales about the walking dead have come down to us in collections of stories known as sagas. These were tales that were recited, but not written down, by *skelds*, the local storytellers, down through the years. They were finally written down by monks in the 13th or 14th century. One of the most famous of these collections is the *Eyrbyggja Saga*, which was probably written in the Icelandic monastery at Helgafell in the early 11th century.

A central tale of one of these collections concerns a warrior by the name of Thorolf Halt-foot who had been greatly feared during his lifetime. He died and was laid to rest in a stone tomb in the countryside, as was the custom for a warrior of his rank. But because of his wild

RIGHT *Icelandic tombs, such as that of Thorolf Halt-foot, had solid pieces of stone erected above them to protect the body.*

lifestyle, death could not restrain him, and it was taken as an ill omen when birds settling on the roof of his tomb fell down dead and cattle grazing close by suddenly went mad and had to be destroyed. Shortly after Thorolf had been put in the tomb, a herdsman was found dead not far from the tomb and it was assumed that Thorolf's cadaver had risen from its grave and was wandering about. The herdsman's body was completely blue and every bone in his body was broken, matching the type of violent assault for which Thorolf was famous.

All through the winter, the dead Viking terrorized the countryside, appearing outside houses in the area and threatening the inhabitants, who had to give him food and drink to make him go away.

ABOVE *Thorolf's corpse was consigned to the earth and shut in by a wall on an almost inaccessible promontory.*

LEFT *Viking warriors were greatly feared in life, but even more in death. Their axes could chop through shields and helmets.*

Thorolf also turned up at the house of the herdsman he had killed, driving the man's wife mad with fear. She died from terror.

The evil corpse was soon joined by several other dead warriors, breaking into houses and causing distress and mayhem. In the end, the Church forced Thorolf's son Arnkel to do something about it. With a posse of neighbors, Arnkel went to his father's tomb, broke it open, removed the body, and placed it on a yoke (wooden frame) between two oxen. The intention was to take the body and dispose of it, but Thorolf's corpse was so heavy that the men and the oxen became exhausted. Instead, they carried his body to a promontory (headland), where they laid it in the earth. Arnkel built a wall around the spot to keep the ghost in. Afterward, this place was avoided by the local people.

Thorolf Halt-foot's name has not been forgotten and still sends a shiver down Scandinavian spines.

"CORNEY"

One of the more bizarre and outrageous ghosts took the form of a poltergeist in late 18th-century Dublin. Although this ghost was never seen, it could speak and offer opinions, many of them extremely rude and unflattering. However, it would never reveal its name, so locals gave it the nickname "Corney."

Corney was believed to live in the coal bin of a grand house somewhere in the Dublin suburbs. Even though it was widely known at the time, both the exact location of the house and the name of the family who lived there are now uncertain. The persons involved are only referred to as "the A-family" in the relevant documents. When the family first moved in, the house had been vacant for a while. The last member of the previous family had died there, as had an old servant whose name was thought to have been Cornelius. Perhaps it was his mischievous ghost that haunted the building.

Shortly after they moved in, the A–family were roused from their beds each night by the noise of something being dragged across the hallway and by sounds outside their bedroom doors that sounded like somebody breaking wind. They put it down to "the old house settling," but soon afterward, the ghost made its presence known in the coal bin. It sounded like a man talking out of an empty barrel and it made rude remarks about the people living in the house. At times, the voice would shift about, sometimes coming from under a bed and sometimes even from the bread bins!

The phantom was certainly a troublesome one. Many of its pranks were directed toward the servants that the A-family had brought with them. From time to time, the specter would throw rotting fish into the center of the kitchen and laugh at those who tried to gather them up. It made cups and crockery disappear, only to turn up again in unexpected places. It tried to make trouble for the senior servants, accusing them of stealing spoons and silverware that it had taken and hidden. It got so bad that two of the serving maids, who slept downstairs,

BELOW *It is difficult to eat meals when a poltergeist has maliciously hidden or damaged all your cutlery and crockery!*

asked if they could be relocated to another room at night because Corney was nipping them and pulling their hair while they slept. But when they moved to another room, the "fold-up" bed on which they slept suddenly sprang to life and Corney's voice was heard to say, "Aha! I'm here before you! I'm everywhere in the house!" The girls fainted clean away.

The ghost was also very rude to anybody who came to visit the family, and it appeared to know a great deal about their private lives. As they sat at tea, it would either pelt them with rotten fruit from some unseen source or reveal embarrassing details about them that it claimed were true.

Then, one day, the disturbances suddenly stopped, and it was thought that Corney had left the house. However, this did not last for long. Corney was soon back – this time breaking crockery and throwing things about to announce its ghostly presence. It had, it said, been away "visiting my daughter that I had when alive. She lives close by!" And after the period of absence, it was more boisterous than ever.

At last, the A-family could stand it no longer and decided to pack up and move. But when prospective buyers came to look around the house, Corney invariably insulted them with sordid details of their private lives. It also sang and whistled in every room in the house, making it impossible for a deal to be struck. However, Corney predicted that the house would eventually be bought by a widow in black, and so it turned out. If the widow was troubled by Corney, she never revealed it.

Although Corney was invisible, one person did see the poltergeist. He was a nine-year-old boy visiting the house. He described the ghost as a naked man, very old, with a great curl on his forehead. Was this truly the manifestation of the awful spirit that had terrified the great house in the Dublin suburbs?

THE FIGURE AT THE GATE

Nowhere in America is as mysterious or eerie as the South Carolina swamplands. The area is difficult to traverse, intercut with rivers and spooky swamps. They lie wreathed in unearthly mists, harboring dark secrets and ghostly reminders of the area's troubled past.

All through this treacherous land lie tiny, shrouded islands, some of which can only be approached by boat. In the 18th and 19th centuries, this was the domain of the so called rice kings, ancient families who made their fortunes growing and exporting rice. They operated large plantations and many of them built grand houses on the tidewater islands or deep inside the swamps. Some of these houses still lie abandoned among the swamp mists and Spanish moss.

Many of these once grand homes have strange and troubled histories.

LEFT *The house on the Litchfield Plantation is a typically beautiful mansion. Today they are often haunted by the rich plantation owners of long ago.*

ABOVE *It is said that a ghostly horseman can be seen riding frantically along the roads near the Litchfield Plantation on Pawleys Island.*

On the swift-flowing Santee River, for instance, stands the elegant Hampton Plantation, founded by the Horry family around 1730, but haunted by the disturbed ghost of one of its later owners, John Henry Rutledge, who hanged himself there after being slighted in love. Farther north lies Peachtree Manor – the Hopsewee Plantation – the original house built by Thomas Lynch Sr. in 1762. His son Thomas Jr. was the youngest signatory of the Declaration of Independence.

Thomas Jr.'s daughter died from yellow fever. Her father went mad and died shortly afterward. The house burned to the ground in 1840. His wailing, deranged phantom is often said to be seen moving mournfully through the South Carolina swamps nearby.

Perhaps one of the most imposing of all the plantation houses is the beautiful Litchfield Plantation on Pawleys Island on the Waccamaw River. The house was originally built in

ABOVE *A figure has been seen outside the gates of Litchfield Plantation, desperately ringing the bell. Is this the ghost of Dr. Massingbird Tucker?*

1740 by landholder Peter Simon from Litchfield in England. The plantation was first owned by the Simon family, but it is another family – the Tuckers, who came to Waccamaw from Bermuda – whose name is predominantly linked with the Litchfield house. They were a colorful family who left their mark on the area – especially John Hyrne Tucker, who ran the plantation between 1797 and 1859. He had nine sons from four marriages and is said to be the father of many more offspring in the surrounding area. On misty nights, a ghostly

LEFT *Hampton Plantation is haunted by the ghost of John Henry Rutledge, who hanged himself because he was rejected in love.*

RIGHT *After the Civil War ended in 1865, Dr. Henry Massingbird Tucker returned to his home, and used his skills to become a prominent Georgetown county physician.*

horseman gallops desperately along the roads of the Waccamaw Neck, arriving at the spot where the old plantation gates once stood. The sound of a bell is heard through the writhing fog and a shadowy figure impatiently paces backward and forward seeking admission. This is said to be the unquiet spirit of Dr. Henry Massingbird Tucker (sometimes spelled Massingberd), who owned Litchfield between 1859 and 1897. He was one of John's sons and was by all accounts as colorful a character as his father.

He served for four years as a volunteer surgeon for the Confederate Army during the Civil War, where he proved his skill with a revolver and the surgeon's knife.

Henry Massingbird Tucker was a complex man. He was very kind to the plantation slaves, who called him "the Ole Doctor." Yet, as a strong Episcopalian, he severely punished those slaves who did not attend church by depriving them of food. He even allowed several slaves to die from starvation.

THE GHOST IN THE GLASS

In many cultures, it is thought that the spirit of a dying person can sometimes become trapped in a mirror or reflective surface, returning as a ghost to torment the living. In Ireland for instance, all mirrors and glasses were kept covered directly after a death and for as long as the body remained in the house.

Buckets of water are often thrown out when someone dies in Ireland for fear that the spirit will otherwise get trapped. This is also the custom in Japan. In an old story from the north of Japan, a young girl visited a shop in a large city to buy herself a present. The shop sold many curios (novel or rare objects) and she was greatly taken by a large mirror. She asked about its origins. The shopkeeper told her that it had come from the former palace of a wealthy man somewhere in the countryside and that it was an extremely rare item.

The girl decided to buy the mirror and paid the shopkeeper

the steep price that he asked. It was when she took it home, however, that her troubles started. She put the mirror in her bedroom close to her bed, but each time she lay down to sleep, she was plagued by strange and terrifying dreams from which she would always wake in a fearful sweat. She continually dreamed that her bedroom was filled with a strange and eerie mist out of which an old man with long and hideous fingernails emerged. He reached for her as she lay in bed and she drew away from him in fright, always waking up just before he actually reached her.

Terrified, she told some of her friends, but they simply laughed at her and said that it was only

RIGHT
In Japan, ghosts are called yurei, which means "faint spirit." The "ghost" that kept the young girl awake took the form of an old man.

a dream brought on by something that she had eaten. The girl was not so sure, and she was convinced that it had something to do with the mirror that she had bought. She tried to make inquiries about it, but the shopkeeper from whom she had bought it knew very little. He did say, however, that he had heard that the palace from which it had been taken had been a very bad place, the home of a sinister old man.

This frightened the girl even more and she went to consult a local wise woman. The woman asked the girl to describe the old man who

came out of the mist. Did he have any feet, for example? The girl said that she had never seen any and he appeared to glide rather than walk.

"Then it is a ghost that you are seeing," answered the old woman. Ghosts in Japan have no feet and are usually only seen from somewhere around the waist upward. "The evil old man's spirit has somehow become trapped in the mirror's glass and now it seeks you for company in its lonely prison. And it will take you with it if you aren't careful. You must have this vile spirit driven away! Speak to a ghost doctor and see if he can help you."

Ghost doctors are Buddhist monks who have been specially trained in exorcism, the driving out of evil spirits. The girl sought one out – a respected old man who came and confirmed what the old woman had said. He burned herbs in front of the mirror and performed certain rituals. As he did so, the mirror screamed and then fell silent.

"The spirit has passed," the ghost doctor advised. "But the mirror is unclean, for the ghost has lodged there. I would advise you to destroy it." And she did, breaking the mirror up and burning it to ashes. She was troubled by ghosts no more.

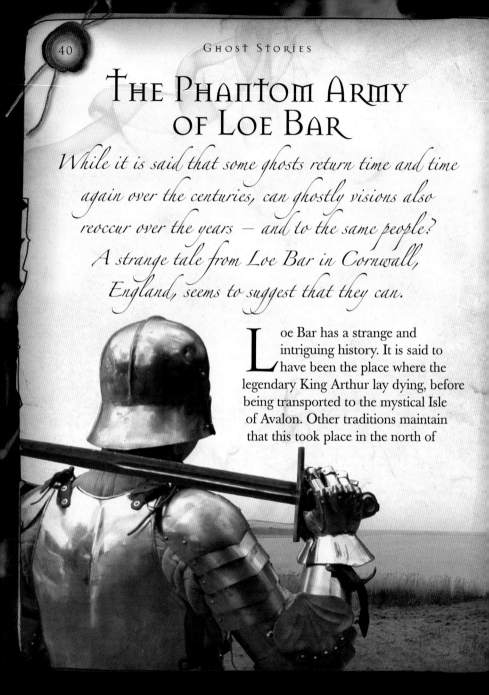

THE PHANTOM ARMY OF LOE BAR

While it is said that some ghosts return time and time again over the centuries, can ghostly visions also reoccur over the years — and to the same people? A strange tale from Loe Bar in Cornwall, England, seems to suggest that they can.

Loe Bar has a strange and intriguing history. It is said to have been the place where the legendary King Arthur lay dying, before being transported to the mystical Isle of Avalon. Other traditions maintain that this took place in the north of

England. Nevertheless, Loe Bar is an eerie place and it is said that Arthur's ghost sometimes haunts the coastline. This belief may form the basis of the following curious tale.

One gloomy evening in August 1936, 16-year-old Stephen Jenkins was exploring a remote and deserted region around Loe Bar before returning to the place where he was vacationing. As he reached the top of a ridge, the boy stopped in astonishment. There, camped in a hollow below, was a horde of medieval warriors dressed in armor and chain-mail surcoats. They were gathered in circles around fires and horses, and the boy had the impression that they were on their way somewhere else and had stopped there to rest. Some of them wore red cloaks, some white, and others black, and these colors were also on their horses. Some of them wore helmets, while others were bareheaded. Some were tending to the horses, while others lounged by the smoking fires. A number of pennants (flags) of various colors fluttered – although there was no breeze – in the center of the camp.

As if aware of the boy on the ridge, one of the knights pointed and said something, but Jenkins could not hear a word. Some of the others started up and the knight stepped forward, half drawing a sword from its sheath. Now frightened, Jenkins turned momentarily, running toward slightly higher ground in order to get away. When he turned back

BELOW *Loe Bar is the ridge of shingle beach that runs alongside a lake called Loe Pool, to which – it is thought – Arthur's sword, Excalibur, was returned as Arthur lay dying.*

to see what was happening, the
hollow below was empty and the
army had vanished. Not even a sign
of their fires remained. Terrified, the
boy ran home.

Such an eerie vision was, in itself,
incredible enough, but there was
more to follow. Thirty-eight years
later, Stephen Jenkins returned to
the same spot, this time on vacation
with his wife. He had always told
her about the strange vision and was
determined to show her where it had

happened. With a map in his hand, he crossed the ridge as before and looked down into the same hollow. There was the army, camped just as they had been all those years before. As Jenkins stood dumbstruck by the vision, he heard his wife gasp. She saw the knights just as clearly as he did! Again, a knight – perhaps the same one – walked to the edge of the group, his hand on his sword. But this time, as he did so, the scene began to fade and the army vanished. Neither Jenkins nor his wife returned to the spot again.

LEFT AND BELOW *Did Jenkins and his wife really see medieval knights and archers? Many people believe that ley lines mark ancient holy spots and that they are lines of energy that bring the past to light. Could that have happened here?*

What was the phantom army? Was it a ghost troop of knights on their way to or from some ancient battle? Some people, including Jenkins himself, have suggested that these may well be fragments of the past, somehow made visible at intersections of ancient, natural force patterns, often known as ley lines. One of these is said to run from nearby Landewednack Church, through Breage Church, to intersect with two other such lines at the village of Townshend.

Is this what "ghosts" really are – no more than little pieces of the past that we can somehow and sometimes see when conditions are right? It is an intriguing suggestion.

THE FLYING DUTCHMAN

The world's oceans remain some of the most mysterious places on Earth, and perhaps the most haunted. The deep and rolling waters hide many secrets. But do phantom vessels continually cross our seas?

There is certainly some evidence that would seem to suggest that this is so. Many sailors, including royalty, have recounted tales of phantom ships glimpsed on stormy nights.

The most famous of all these phantoms is that of the ship, the *Flying Dutchman*. This is an enduring legend that has even been the theme of an opera by Richard Wagner and has recently come to prominence once more in the sequels to the hit movie *Pirates of the Caribbean*.

The story of the vessel varies from storyteller to storyteller, but there are certain similarities in each version.

It is said, for instance, that the captain was an arrogant Dutchman (his name is sometimes given as Falkenberg, Ramhout van Damm, or Heinrich Van der Decken). He was in command of either a tea clipper (ship) or a Dutch man-of-war (warship). The ship was making heavy weather of rounding the Cape of Good Hope, a notorious area for storms, when the captain cursed

RIGHT *The Devil plays cards with the ship's captain, for the chance to win his soul.*

God and said that he would round the Cape and make port if it took until eternity. It is said that God granted his wish and so the vessel is still sailing, trying to land until the Day of Judgement comes.

That is the basis of the story, but over the years, different details have been added. For instance, it is said that the Captain sits on board his vessel playing cards with the Devil for his own soul – a wager he can never win. Some people warn that to see the phantom vessel – which, according to some stories, only appears off the Cape of Good Hope, but in others it is seen all over the world's oceans – is a sinister omen. To others, it is simply a phantom vessel. Sightings of it have, however, continued up until modern times.

One recorded sighting took place on July 11, 1881, when the British naval vessel *HMS Inconstant* was making its way along the Australian coast from Melbourne to Sydney. In the light of the early morning, two midshipmen saw a strange vessel emerge out of the drifting mists. It looked like an old-time

RIGHT *Many have claimed to have seen ghostly ships through the dense sea mists. Could one of these have been the* Flying Dutchman*?*

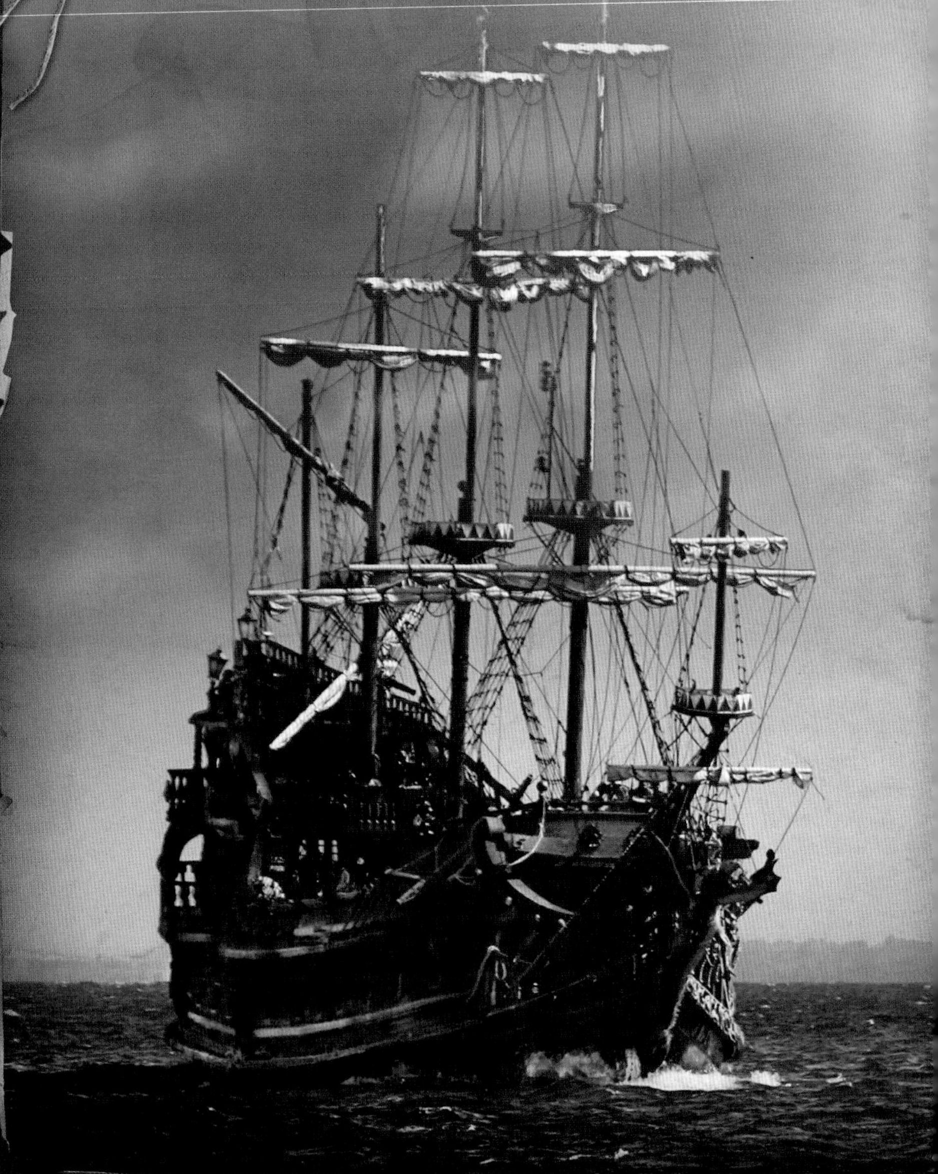

LEFT *Sightings in the 19th and 20th centuries reported that the* Flying Dutchman *was glowing with a ghostly light.*

sailing ship with torn sails and tall masts. She was surrounded in an eerie reddish light that made her "spars, sails, and masts" stand out in strong relief. To the amazement of the young men, the ship faded back into the mist and the eerie light was extinguished. There remained "no vestige or any sign whatever of any material ship." The young midshipmen were extremely sure of what they had seen, and their word is not to be doubted for they were Prince George (later King George V of England) and his brother, Prince Albert Victor.

But just who was the "Flying Dutchman," and why did he give his name to the ship? There was a historical figure that was associated with both the sea and with ghosts, although he was not exactly a Dutchman. His name was Bernard Fokke (1600–1641) and he was a Frisian-born captain for the Dutch East India Company, carrying tea to Europe from the Far East. He became known for the speed of his trips between Java and the port of Rotterdam, earning him the German nickname Fliegender Hollander ("Flying Dutchman"). So swift were his journeys that it was assumed that he had supernatural help and was connected to the Devil. Indeed, his ship was allegedly seen, still racing, with Fokke at the helm in 1678, 30 years after his death.

So is the *Flying Dutchman* a ghost or merely a legend – only the endless, rolling seas have the answer!

THE SPECTRAL HOUND

Many people are familiar with The Hound of the Baskervilles, written in 1901 by Sir Arthur Conan Doyle, and featuring his great, fictional detective Sherlock Holmes. But is the story based in fact?

The legend of the hound tells the story of the wicked nobleman, Hugo Baskerville, pursuing his young wife across the bleak Dartmoor countryside in southern England before cornering her in some ruins. There, he plans to ravish and murder her. He is suddenly attacked by a large hound that tears him to pieces for his evil crime. Since then, so the story goes, his evil spirit haunts Dartmoor in the guise of a spectral hound. It is this murderous canine that Holmes and his companion Watson have to track down in order to lift the curse of the Baskervilles. But is this story true?

During a trip to Dartmoor, Conan Doyle probably heard about Richard Cabell, the 17th-century squire of Buckfastleigh, in Devon, from one of his journalist friends, Bertram Fletcher Robinson of the *Daily Express*. By any standards, Cabell was a treacherous man. In 1647, he is recorded as being heavily fined for siding with the Royalists

RIGHT *In the story, Sherlock Holmes finds out that the ghostly hound is terrifyingly real!*

during the English Civil War. He showed no loyalty, immediately renouncing his former allegiance to King Charles I, and declared for the opposing Parliamentary forces, which enabled him to keep his lands around Buckfastleigh.

Described as "monstrously evil," legend says that Cabell married several times, each time for land and property, and that he even went so far as to sell his soul to the Devil. In life, he loved nothing better than drinking, gambling, and hunting. Indeed, he kept a pack of hunting dogs that were "the terror of Dartmoor," so vicious were they. Cabell married a young and beautiful local girl, but one night, during a drunken party, he lost her in a wager to one of his drinking companions. Rather than face such an indignity, the girl fled across the moors and was pursued by Cabell and his hunting dogs, before being cornered in the ruins of an old abbey. As her pursuers approached, she prayed and her prayers were answered. One of the massive dogs, with which the girl had a special affinity, suddenly turned on the wicked squire as he dismounted, and tore out his throat.

The story is probably a fabrication, and when Cabell died on July 5, 1677, he was laid to rest in Buckfastleigh churchyard. The locals claimed that a pack of ghostly hounds raced through the skies, and his body is laid under a great stone to prevent it from rising again. He was deeply involved in the black arts, so death might not have been a deterrent for him, and it is said that his ghost haunts Dartmoor in the shape of the black dog that killed him. This grisly tale may have inspired Conan Doyle's story.

It is thought that Conan Doyle named his character, Sir Henry Baskerville, after a coachman named Harry Baskerville, who first introduced Conan Doyle to the misty hollows and bogs of Dartmoor. The description of Baskerville Hall is said to have been modeled on Cromer Hall in Norfolk, where a devil dog named Black Shuck haunts the countryside. This is said to be a demon or the ghost of an evil sorcerer and has been recorded in the area since 1577. This legend may also have influenced Doyle.

So be careful if you hear a distant howl on a dark night – who knows what sort of spectral hound may be waiting for you!

BELOW *Cromer Hall in Norfolk is the atmospheric inspiration for Conan Doyle's Baskerville Hall.*

Haunted Places

There are some places in the world that people would be advised to avoid, as they are said to belong only to the dead. Maybe you know of such a place — a closed-up room, an old abandoned house, a ruined church, a dark grove of trees, or a sinister graveyard. Many such places have an aura about them — a sinister feeling, a sensation of dread or evil — that often chills us to the very core of our being. Could it be a ghost passing by? Is that unexplained noise the voice of a phantom or some specter making itself known? Step with us now, if you dare, across the threshold of another world and see what is lurking there.

BORLEY RECTORY

Once described as "the most haunted house in England," Borley Rectory in Essex had a strange and troubled history. Although it is no longer standing, it still casts a long and eerie shadow and has a ghostly legend.

Borley was originally built in 1862 by the Reverend Henry Dawson Ellis Bull to house his family of 14 children. According to legend, it was built on the site of a Benedictine monastery founded in 1362. Here, a certain monk was allegedly killed for having an affair with a nun from a nearby convent. The nun herself was supposedly starved to death.

Throughout their time at Borley, the Bull family claimed to have seen and heard many strange things. Unexplained footsteps, noises, and voices were regular occurrences, and strange figures were often seen close to the house. On July 28, 1900, four of the girls saw a nun standing in the rectory garden in the twilight, but when they tried to speak to her, the nun vanished.

Henry Bull died in 1892 and his son Harry became the Rector of Borley. The strange events continued, but now a phantom carriage was often seen driving up to the rectory. Things got so bad that some of the unmarried girls had to move out and live in the nearby Chilton Lodge.

When Harry died in 1927, he was succeeded as Rector by the Reverend Guy Eric Smith who moved in the following year. As

BELOW *As well as eerie noises, voices, and strange figures, a phantom carriage was sometimes seen near the house.*

Mrs. Smith was cleaning out a cupboard, she unexpectedly found a parcel containing the skull of a young girl. At once, the ghostly phenomena started again with a vengeance – knockings, footsteps, servants' bells ringing (even though their ropes had been cut), and the phantom carriage, which appeared more frequently.

The Smiths contacted the *Daily Mirror* newspaper, hoping to be put in contact with the Society for Psychical Research. The newspaper, however, sent a reporter there on June 10, 1929, together with the self-styled psychic investigator Harry Price. Almost as soon as he arrived, poltergeist activity began all through the house, and Mrs. Smith strongly suspected that he had something to do with the activity.

The Smiths left Borley on July 14, 1929, and were replaced by the Reverend Lionel Foyster, a relative of the Bulls, his wife Marianne, and

BELOW *New to the rectory, Mrs. Smith discovered a young girl's skull in a cupboard, triggering the start of much spooky activity in the house again.*

their adopted daughter, Adelaide. Once again, the ghostly phenomena increased and continued until around 1937. Many psychics were called to the house and all of them suspected Marianne of being behind many of the happenings. Later, she would admit to using the "ghostly visitations" as a cover for her affair with a lodger, Frank Peerless. The Foysters finally left because of Lionel's ill-health.

In May 1937, Harry Price took a year's lease on Borley in order to carry out some psychic experiments there. One of his assistants, Helen Glanville, conducted a planchette séance, using a set of letters carved in wood that resembled a Ouija board. She claimed to have contacted two spirits. One was of a French nun, Marie Lairre, who said she had been murdered there in 1667. The other was named Sunex Amures, who stated that they would burn the rectory down on March 27, 1938 (but failed to do so).

However, on March 27, 1939, the new owner, Captain W. H. Gregson, accidentally overturned an oil lamp as he was unpacking some boxes. The resulting blaze destroyed much of the building.

ABOVE *Harry Price first visited Borley in 1929 and carried out psychic experiments there during the year 1937.*

Borley Rectory made Harry Price famous as England's leading ghost hunter, and he wrote a book about his experiences there (though many aspects of the book have been challenged by other investigators). The BBC also commissioned a program on Borley, but this was abandoned after threats of legal action from Marianne Foyster.

In 1944, Borley Rectory was demolished. Nevertheless, it is still considered to have been one of the world's most haunted houses.

ABBEY OF LOST SOULS

Set deep in a gloomy French valley and surrounded by a dense beech forest, Mortemer Abbey, Normandy's earliest Cistercian foundation, is a sinister place.

The abbey was founded in 1134 by Henry I, the son of William the Conqueror, on a stretch of bogland known in Latin as *mortuum mare*, meaning "sea of the dead." In the 15th century, it housed more than 200 monks and followed the highest religious ideals – chastity, poverty, and rejection of the world. But its great wealth caused the monks to fall into petty squabbling, greed, lust, and assassination, and by 1790 there were only four brothers living there. They were murdered by revolutionaries and their blood was mixed with wine from the abbey cellars. It was around this time that Mortemer acquired the nickname of "the Abbey of Lost Souls."

There have been many disturbing stories concerning the abbey. A room, named the Pink Room, was said to be the prison of Henry I's daughter, Matilda, for five years. Her ghost, dressed in white, is said to haunt the grounds of Mortemer. If she is seen wearing black gloves, it is a sure sign of death, but if they are white, it signifies a wedding or a birth. But she is not the only phantom that haunts the abbey. Shadowy monks have often been seen gliding, pictures and mirrors are turned to face the walls by unseen hands, and footsteps and breathing are still frequently heard.

At the end of the 19th century, the abbey was acquired by Monsieur Delarue, who lived there with his family. They were haunted by eerie chanting, doors banging, and heavy footsteps. Their cars, although kept in a shed, were mysteriously found covered in a strange white dust. The Delarues had the place exorcized in 1921 – but left soon afterward.

RIGHT *The ghost of Matilda haunts the abbey. Her clothes are said to signify either death, a birth, or a wedding. She is not the only ghost to have taken up residence in the abbey.*

LEAP CASTLE

Leap Castle has often been considered one of Europe's most sinister places. Once the stronghold of the O'Carroll clan, it has a blood-soaked history.

The castle takes its name from the original rulers of the area, the O'Bannons. They later became tenants of the O'Carrolls, the "Dark Princes of Ely," who were a fierce clan who controlled part of the Irish midlands. Legend says that the Dark Princes agreed to let the O'Bannons remain as chiefs if one of their champions could leap a particular distance. The champion jumped, but failed. It is said that the O'Carrolls used his blood to mix the mortar for Leap.

In the mid-1500s, following the death of one of the O'Carrolls, a fierce family war broke out. Leap was now the stronghold of Tadhg O'Carroll, one of the most vicious of the warlords. His elder brother Thaddeus MacFir O'Carroll, who was a priest, tried to make peace with other members of the family, but Tadhg was opposed to this. One evening, he cut Thaddeus's throat as he knelt in prayer. To kill a man as he talked to God was both a sin and a blasphemy, and so when Tadhg himself was killed shortly after, his spirit – a cross between a ghost and a vampire – was denied entry to the afterlife and still haunts the Bloody Chapel in the Castle. Tadhg is also credited with killing 40 members of the rival O'Mahon clan by bricking them up in a deep dungeon. Their wailing ghosts can still be heard from time to time.

After the O'Carroll era, Leap passed into the hands of the Darbys and it is said that one – a madman – hid a fortune there after murdering several servants. The treasure has never been found, but as night falls and a ghostly light shines from the window of the Bloody Chapel, would you go to look for it?

RIGHT *The mysterious Leap Castle has a long and disturbing history. Many people with sinister backgrounds have lived there.*

THE WOLF'S SEAT

There are many places all over Scotland steeped in ancient evil, perhaps none more sinister than Spynie Palace near Elgin in Morayshire.

Although it was the seat of the Bishops of Moray for nearly 500 years, the building's dark and hollow shell speaks of a troubled, sinister history.

One of its most infamous residents was the terrible Alexander Stewart, who was the Earl of Buchan and brother to King Robert III of Scotland. He was also known as "the Wolf of Badenoch," and in 1397 his outlaw troops (known as ketterens) torched Elgin, looting the cathedral as part of the Wolf's dispute with Alexander Burr, Bishop of Moray. Although the Wolf held Spynie for no more than a year, his specter is still reputedly seen about the ancient palace, leaning over a rail on the David's Tower section of the building and gazing down on the people below with an evil intent.

The Tower itself is mysteriously haunted, and even today a number of visitors have reported seeing a hairy face glaring at them from

LEFT *Intrigued by the history and mystery surrounding it, visitors still visit Spynie Palace.*

certain windows in the upper stories. Although many of the inner walls and vaults have long since collapsed, there are still almost-hidden rooms, passages, and dark recesses to the east of the tower that greatly lend themselves to a ghostly atmosphere.

A woman is often seen sitting to the right of the tower. And on some of the upper passages, visitors have been overcome by strong nausea caused by a heavy, unpleasant stench. Spookily, all that needs to be done is to step aside and say "excuse me" and the feeling passes, as does the unseen entity. A mysterious skull sometimes

ABOVE *Visitors to the eerie palace could be met with a sighting of a strange figure, a white mist – or an unpleasant smell!*

appears in photographs taken inside the tower, as does the outline of a lion, one of the bishops' pets. Perhaps the most frightening specter is the man-sized column of white mist that often drifts threateningly toward visitors and has been known to knock some of them over.

Despite its chilling reputation, Spynie Palace continues to draw visitors from all over the world and, mixed with the often eerie atmosphere, the palace boasts a certain charm that both captivates and enthrals them.

WAVERLY HILLS SANATORIUM

Sometimes described as "the most haunted building in America," the Waverly Hills Sanatorium is a sinister and threatening building. And yet, as haunted places go, it is fairly recent, only dating back to 1910.

In 1883, Major Thomas H. Hayes purchased the land and established a small school in Louisville, KY. He employed Miss Lizzie Lee Harris as teacher. She was a great fan of Sir Walter Scott's "Waverley" novels and christened the area with that name – one which Hayes himself liked. When the second "e" was dropped from the title is unknown, but by 1900, the name Waverly Hills was established.

In 1911, Jefferson County was ravaged by the "White Plague," a phrase used to describe pulmonary tuberculosis. The authorities in Louisville decided to build a new hospital to deal specifically with the outbreak. Work was hampered by financial wrangling, and in

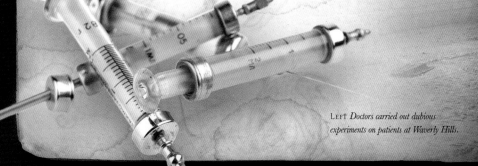

LEFT *Doctors carried out dubious experiments on patients at Waverly Hills.*

that same year patients from several surrounding hospitals were temporarily transferred to a new building at Waverly Hills. This subsequently became a permanent hospital and was extended to include experimentation centers set up to find ways of dealing with the disease. Even today, legend says that there are secret laboratories hidden away in the building where doctors experimented on dying patients in hideous ways in order to try to find a cure. Tuberculosis affected many of the inmates mentally, and

there were special areas known as "madhouses" where such unfortunates were detained. Today, some of those areas are considered to be especially haunted by the spirits of former patients who wail and gibber along unlighted corridors or in long-abandoned wards.

But the most persistent legend concerns Room 502. It was allegedly here in 1928 that the body of a young nurse was found hanging from a ceiling beam. Why she committed suicide is unknown, but she was said to have been

BELOW *Are those patients who were mentally affected by tuberculosis and kept in the areas known as madhouses still haunting the corridors and wards?*

unmarried and pregnant. Later, in 1932, another nurse jumped to her death from the roof of the building after spending some time in Room 502. Those who have visited it say that a noticeable air of depression pervades the entire room and affects all those who enter.

There are also stories of a "death tunnel," a chute by which the doctors at the hospital secretly disposed of the dead bodies of those they had experimented upon. It was alleged that the bodies were simply dropped into a chamber in the basement. However, there was indeed a tunnel along which bodies were taken on gurneys by the doctors in order to avoid disturbing other patients and preserve the morale of the hospital.

Waverly Hills ceased to be a tubercular hospital in 1962 when new cures for the disease became available. Renamed the Woodhaven Geriatric Hospital, it was charged with the care of the elderly. It was a place for those elderly patients with special mental problems, and became a sort of "asylum for the elderly." In 1981, it was closed amid claims of patient abuse and it has not reopened as a hospital since.

However, its ghosts refuse to go away. One of the most frequently seen ghosts is an old woman with long, straggly hair and wild, insane eyes, wearing a bloodstained ward tunic with metal cuffs. She is said to have been a particularly violent "inmate" who had to be continually restrained and still wanders the passages waiting for her family to come and take her home.

There are plans to turn the old sanatorium into a four-star hotel, but these are at an early stage. In the meantime, the only "guests" in the old building are its phantoms of former times.

ABOVE RIGHT *A nurse committed suicide in the infamous Room 502.* BELOW *The cursed Waverly Hills building.*

THE HAUNTED MILITARY BASE

Over the years, many military installations have been subjected to some sort of haunting, and armed forces in many countries have claimed to have been troubled by ghosts. The panzer base at Kaiserslautern, near Stuttgart in Germany, seems to have experienced more than its fair share of ghostly phenomena.

The panzer (a german army tank, shown right) base is still a working barracks and home to the 21st Theater Support Command, which offers all sorts of logistic support for military initiatives within the North Atlantic Treaty Organization (NATO). The town of Kaiserslautern is an extremely old one and was one of the settlements under the protection of Frederick Barbarossa, King of Germany and Holy Roman Emperor (1155–1198). It is said that on the site where the base now stands, Frederick built a monastery that later became an important house for the Premonstatensian (Norbertine) Order.

Many serving at the barracks can believe this, as the shapes of monks with their heads bowed in contemplation, are often seen there.

Late at night, the sound of chanting is heard coming from the various sheds where tanks are housed. Those working in the offices late at night have also heard the sound of footsteps coming and going along the staircases, and from time to time the lights have been inexplicably switched off and on.

The sound of papers rustling and low voices come from some of the offices when there is no one there, although it is not possible to hear what is said. It is thought that these sounds may stem from World War II when the place was used as a central base for panzers. Much of the activity comes from the third floor where many of the war offices were sited, and today's staff often refuse to go there after dark.

And so, even in a still-active and mechanized military base, the spirits of the departed are still in charge as soon as daylight fades.

BELOW *Lots of unexplained spooky phenomena take place at night at the tank base at Kaiserslautern.*

SHRIEVES HOUSE

Number 40 Sheep Street, in Stratford, England is the oldest surviving structure in Stratford, dating back to the 16th century. It has survived plague, fire, and civil war.

There is even a legend that the house was visited by William Shakespeare. Its name, Shrieves House, is taken from its builder William Shrieve, who lived in the time of Henry VIII. Very little is known about him. It is said that he was an archer and perhaps a military man, but that he was also something of an eccentric. Beyond that, he is a mystery. However, there is a real legacy of ghosts in the house that he built.

At the back of the building is a large converted barn, and it is here that ghostly activity seems at its worst. This comes mostly in the form of sensations – a sense of breathlessness or intense claustrophobia – and many visitors have thought that they were being smothered or forcibly confined. Occasionally, too, the figure of a huge man, in 16th-century dress, is seen on the upper floors. He carries an ax and the figure is thought to be Shrieve himself, objecting to anyone entering the house that he built.

At a window on the main staircase, the specter of an old lady signals with a candle to some long-dead person outside, and some of the rooms are said to be haunted by an English Civil War soldier who hanged himself on the landing. Various mediums who have attempted to conduct séances in the building have been overwhelmed by the sense of psychic energy and evil that infests the place.

In February 2004, the house was the site for an episode of Living TV's *Most Haunted* and, not surprisingly, was voted the scariest place!

RIGHT *A figure wielding an ax can sometimes be seen on the upper floors of Shrieves House. Could the figure be the ghost of Shrieve, the man who built the house?*

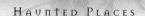

WINCHESTER MYSTERY HOUSE

Maybe one of the strangest buildings in America is also possibly the most tragic. The Winchester Mystery House, in the Santa Clara Valley in California, stands today as a testament to the loneliness, grief, and fear of one woman whose tragic story resonates down the ages.

The story of the house's peculiar and tormented owner begins in September 1839, with the birth of Sarah Pardee into a wealthy family in New Haven, Connecticut. She grew into a young woman of elegance and charm, and was much courted by local gentlemen. The man to whom she was attracted, however, was William

ABOVE *This is the only known portrait of Sarah Winchester. After her husband died, she built the Winchester Mystery House for the spirits that haunted her.*

Wirt Winchester, son of Oliver Winchester, a wealthy Connecticut shirt manufacturer and businessman. In 1857, William took over the Volcanic Repeater Rifle firm and began to manufacture firearms. This was timely, for in 1861 the American Civil War broke out and Winchester's product, the Henry Repeater, became the favorite weapon of the Union army.

LEFT *The Winchester Mystery House has a grand appearance from the outside, but inside, the house is a confusing assortment of passages, corridors, staircases, and rooms.*

Sarah and William were married on September 30, 1862, as William's business and fortune grew. On July 15, 1866, Sarah gave birth to a baby daughter, but the infant suffered from a congenital illness and died a few days later. Sarah never got over her death, but further tragedy was to strike in the coming years. On March 7, 1881, William also died after a long and wasting illness – pulmonary tuberculosis.

His death, on top of that of her child, devastated Sarah, who consulted a spiritualist medium to try to contact her husband. The medium gave her a chilling message – her family was under a curse from the ghosts of those who had been killed using Winchester rifles. In order to placate these angry spirits, she must give up her life in Connecticut and venture toward "the setting sun." In an ordained place, she was to build a dwelling to house all the phantoms that would become her life's work. She could never stop building – if she did, she would die.

Taking the medium's word literally and with a vast fortune at her disposal, Sarah headed west. In 1884, she reached the Santa Clara

Valley, where she came across a grand, half-built mansion. A retired medical man, Dr. Caldwell, was in the process of building a six-bedroom house for himself and his family, but he abandoned the project when Sarah offered him a massive sum for it. She then continued to build the house herself, in order to house the spirits of the dead who she believed tormented her.

Sarah did not stop building until she died. She employed armies of carpenters, masons, and journeymen who continually added to the building over the years.

Sarah watched over the architectural plans herself, claiming that she was being guided by the ghosts who had already inhabited the building. Rooms were added in a haphazard fashion and staircases were constructed that went nowhere, while secret cupboards and recesses contributed to the chaos. All the passages and corridors interconnected and many doubled back on themselves. This, Sarah said, was to confuse the ghosts so that they could not "get to her and harm her." How she found her way around the house is unknown, but it is thought that she only lived in certain rooms. Only two mirrors were allowed in the house because she believed that the ghosts could not look at their own reflections.

Sarah also had an obsession with the number 13 – many rooms had 13 windows, the windows had 13 panes, and all of the staircases except one had flights of 13 steps. There were 47 fireplaces but many more chimneys – so that "the ghosts could come and go." Eventually, the house reached seven stories and was a warren of corridors, stairs, and rooms. Somewhere in the center of this, Sarah lived with a few servants. She was virtually a recluse.

In 1906, California was hit by a massive earthquake that almost destroyed the house. Sarah began to rebuild, but she died on September 4, 1922, with the work still ongoing. It has been said that the building has 160 known rooms, though this may not be entirely accurate. The house has since been declared a California National Landmark.

Was Sarah tormented by ghosts or simply mad with grief? Perhaps the answer lies in the building.

Right *Despite the grand size of the house, Sarah Winchester only lived in a few of the rooms – the rest were left for the ghosts.*

THE BLACK HAG OF SHANAGOLDEN

Located in a shallow valley about two miles (three kilometers) east of the village of Shanagolden in County Limerick, Ireland, the ruins of old St. Katherine's Augustinian Convent are almost swamped by the surrounding vegetation.

The ruins of the medieval nunnery have an extremely sinister aspect about them, and rightly so, for the foundation is said to have had a dubious history.

Founded in 1298, St. Katherine's was, at that time, one of the biggest abbeys in the area and was a place of worship for the local Fitzgerald chieftains. According to legend, during the wars that ripped this region apart throughout the 16th and 17th centuries, the wife of one of the Earls of Desmond was seriously wounded. Her husband took her to the abbey and then returned to the battle. He effectively left her to die, placing her unconscious body in a coffin. But the lady was not dead

and legends say that she woke up in the grave. Her final screams are said to ring around the ruins each day as night falls.

But it is the way in which St. Katherine's convent was dissolved that gives the place its most eerie ghost. Tradition says that the order to dissolve the convent came from the Pope himself and that it was because the nuns there practiced witchcraft. They were led by a reportedly "evil" abbess, the superior of the nuns, who became known locally as "the Black Abbess" or "the Black Hag."

When the convent was dissolved and the nuns moved elsewhere, she stayed on in the deteriorating

building and was frequently seen gathering herbs and roots in the countryside. The abbess supposedly made her living as a witch and fortune-teller, working for the nobles in the surrounding countryside.

A passing traveler found her dead one morning, seated in the ruined cloister which became known as "the Black Hag's Cell." She still refuses to leave St. Katherine's. Her ghost is seen drifting through the ancient ruins. Perhaps it is advisable to stay well away from the old abbey, especially after dark!

ABOVE *Was a hastily dug grave the last resting place of the wife of one of the Earls of Desmond?*

BELOW *Little remains of the old convent, though screams are said to ring around the ruins.*

GLOSSARY

Afterlife
A realm that lies beyond death. It is given as the abode of ghosts, angels, and demons.

Cadaver
A dead body. Sometimes refers specifically to a corpse that has been animated by a spirit.

Demon
A fallen angel or evil force that is generally believed to stand against Mankind.

Elemental
A supernatural force which comprised one of the four natural elements – earth, water, fire, and air.

Escapologist
A professional artist who entertains by escaping from seemingly impossible situations.

Exorcism
The casting out of demons and ghosts.

Ghost
The restless spirit of a dead person. Also sometimes called an apparition.

Illusionist
A person who can create the semblance of something which is not actually real.

Lares
Spirits in ancient Roman folk belief which protected households, fields, and boundaries. They may have once been former gods.

Lemures
Very powerful and dangerous forces in ancient Roman belief, such as a vengeful ghost.

Ley Lines
Lines of elemental power that are said to run across the countryside between certain points in the landscape.

Magician
A practitioner of the supernatural arts. One who can draw down spirits and ghosts. Also sometimes called a sorcerer.

Mane
A vindictive ghost described by the Roman writer Plotinus and by St. Augustine, which attacked people while they were asleep.

Medium
An object or person through which a ghost can communicate with the living or make its wishes known.

Ouija Board
A flat board marked with letters, numbers, and other symbols that is used for communicating with spirits or ghosts.

Poltergeist
A noisy and disruptive ghost which is usually invisible. From two German words "poltern" (to rumble or make noise) and "geist" (spirit).

Séance
An attempt to communicate with the dead. The word originally comes from the French, meaning "seat." Also called a "contact session."

Spirit
The soul or essence of a person that can sometimes appear after death. The word comes from the Latin *spiritus,* meaning "breath."

Spirit-seer
One who has the ability to see spirits and ghosts.

INDEX

Continues over the page

ÍNDEX CONTINUED

ACKNOWLEDGMENTS

Marshall Editions would like to thank the following agencies for supplying images for inclusion in this book:

t = top   **b** = bottom   **c** = center   **r** = right   **l** = left

Cover Credits: Front cover design by Tim Scrivens; Jacket photography: Shutterstock

Pages: 1 Corbis/Mike Agliolo; **8tl** Corbis/Bettmann; **12** Bridgeman/Alinari; **13t** Corbis/Gianni Dagli Orti; **13b** Alamy/Paris Pierce; **14** Mary Evans Picture Library; **15** Mary Evans Picture Library; **16** TopFoto/Charles; **17** Alamy/Paris Pierce; **23** Alamy/Timewatch Images; **25** Alamy/The Photolibrary Wales; **26** Dave Donaldson/Alamy; **27** Corbis/Jim Richardson; **31** Corbis/Barry Lewis/In Pictures, Corbis/Whisson/Jordan; **32** Litchfield Plantation/Public Domain; **33** Corbis/Stapleton Collection; **35** Corbis/Medford Historical Society Collection; **36** Corbis/Southern Stock/Blend Images; **37** Corbis/Southern Stock/Blend Images; **42-43** Corbis/Stapleton Collection; **44** Alamy/Valerie Garner; **49** Alamy/Lebrecht Music and Arts Photo Library; **50-51** stavros1/Public Domain; **57** The Bridgman Art Library; **59** Corbis/Gervais Courtellemont/National Geographic Society; **61** Alamy/The Marsden Archive; **63** Public Domain; **72t** Alamy/Interfoto **72b** Corbis/Richard T. Nowitz; **73** Corbis/Bettmann; **75** Corbis/Richard T. Nowitz; **77t** Corbis/Lt. Rothberg; **77b** JohnArmagh/Public Domain